When the journey is over, dive into what it did for you, how it made you feel, and the human you became because of it. We must go where our boundaries feel tested. It is the only way we can find out what fits and what doesn't in our new life. I am thankful for the moments that tested me and the places that made me reach further inside of my soul to figure out if I could or if it was all in my head to begin with.

-karnes-

<u>*UTAH TO TEXAS*</u>

<u>*-A Poet's Journey-*</u>

1:16PM
10.19.23
Red Journal
TX

Taking time getting back into the routine I got away

from is me realizing how miserable I once was.

Traveling does heal, even if it is chaos, it is needed

chaos. There will always be a time when you feel

as though you are at your limit, and that is when

you need to give just a little more to end up where

you belong, where you deserve to be.

12:28PM
10.21.23
Red Journal
TX

May your fears only inspire you and give your soul

the push it needs. Lean into the flames. Allow them

to light your way. Allow them to guide you in whatever

direction the wind blows its colors for you to see

your next step, your next victory.

12:29PM
10.21.23
Red Journal
TX

Become enamored with your own life. Set your goals.

Set your affirmations. Dance with the moon and her

light. Be aware of the distractions. May peace kiss your

sorrows. May serenity keep your wounds cleaned

and loved. You are here to be more than the face you

see in the mirror, more than the shadow you can

oftentimes be. Prepare yourself for the war, and the rest

will be the life you dreamt about as a child, wondering

if anything in life comes easy.

1:44PM
10.21.23
Red Journal
TX

Take your chances. Make your efforts known.

Speak everything and all your desires into existence.

Your future is worth the past it took for you to be here.

Do not let the child you once were down because you

are afraid of failing. Nothing ever happens without

that outcome happening first.

1:56PM
10.21.23
Red Journal
TX

Love has left me, and maybe for good this time.

I wish I had another morning to wake up to you.

I wish I had one more kiss to give, and for you

to kiss me back like you once did.

11:50PM
10.22.23
Red Journal
TX

Taking time for yourself and making time for

your own needs is what separated those who

know they are from those who die never knowing.

1:52PM
10.22.23
Red Journal
TX

Love me as I am. Take these burdens from the

bones and bury them in your gardens. I had

never seen the sun until I walked with your flowers.

I had never known of light until you stepped in front

of everything I had been running away from.

12:34PM
10.23.23
Red Journal
TX

I would give up my own heart for you to feel

everything I have since meeting you. I hope

you know how much you are loved. I hope you

know how much I loved you when I said it the

first time, and then the last time when you

walked away. In my mind, I believe I can still

love you, but my attempts would be futile now

compared to who I was when I never

wanted anyone other than you.

12:42PM
10.23.23
Red Journal
TX

As I write the last poem in this journal,

I hope it brings peace and clarity as it did

for me. Take your own love and move on

from those who cannot love you back.

Your life is worth more than being shown

by someone else it isn't. You deserve to

know how it feels to wake up never questioning

if the soul next to you loves you more today.

3:44PM   10.18.23   Texas

Yesterday, we watched GetUp! and Pat's show until 11AM. Asa drove us back to Park City and carried his drone again. It was not nearly as packed as the Saturday we went. We walked to the Eating Establishment, which was half-way up Main St. I had stone oats, quinoa, and yogurt with fruit. Asa had eggs, pancakes, and bacon. Dad had a Caesar salad. Total bill was eighty-five dollars after the tip. No way I could afford PCU, but Italy I could. It is crazy how that works. After that, Asa wanted to take me to a coffee shop, La Niche, which was down at the bottom of Main St. It was a coffee shop in the back of a store. It already had Christmas decorations and a tree out. I ordered my Americano and it was an excellent mix the woman made. She was Italian. Go figure. After that, Asa stopped at the Miner's hospital, which is on the way out of the town. He took his drone out and got some insane shots of the surrounding area. Before that he took us to Guardsman's Pass. The leaves had fallen off most of the trees, but the valley and outlook was nothing short of inspiring. That part of Utah has a magical way of making you feel incredibly small. It is beyond humbling to take in. We all three took photos and that is when we went to get some food. After the drone shot, we stopped a few more times and Asa made some videos with it. The fall there is worth the trip if you can make it, I miss it and have missed it every single day since I have left. We got back to the house and finished laundry. Dad and I packed for the trip home. We watched Sportscenter and some of the baseball pregame before leaving for the airport around 6:43PM. The sunset was not as spectacular as the sunrise, but the waning crescent moon was placed against the perfectly fixated pink starburst of a sky. We arrived at the airport by 7PM. Thankfully, there was a shuttle there as we were walking up. Without Asa being a flight attendant, this trip would not have happened, and definitely would have been a million times more difficult to create and have it turn out the way it did. We were able to use the employee shuttle, elevator. Asa was able to get us standby tickets basically for free. My typewriter got pulled again for security. They laughed at it being an authentic one. They could not believe someone still used them. It took an additional ten to fifteen minutes to get through security each time because of it, but I have stories and memories of what it did for the trip. We got to the gate which was at the very end of Gate A. Asa stayed with us until the plane was good to go and we were guaranteed a seat. He has a Delta app that tells him how full the flights are, so before we left, it had fifty or so open seats. Unheard of for that many to be available. Just like the rest of the trip after Como and Nesso, everything went as smoothly as humanly possible. It all worked out. The boarding began at 8:30PM. We were checked in around 9PM. We said our goodbyes to Asa and got seated in comfort plus. We took off at 9:10PM It was the shortest two hours of my life. I played a few games on the tv screen. Dad watched a movie on someone else's screen in first class. I honestly have never been a part of something for two hours that felt like thirty minutes, if that. We landed at 12:20AM and got off the plane. We then made our way to ground transportation and again, it worked out perfectly as the airport shuttle was there and took off as soon as we were seated in it. We got to the garage within ten minutes, then took a van to my car. It felt so fucking amazing driving again. 18 days with your vehicle parked there is $211. The tax on it alone was forty dollars. Well worth it considering the trip of a lifetime that we had just made. We got on the road around 1AM. I drove 80-90mph plus on the way back. We stopped at a convenience store and got a red bull and water, then made it back to the house before 3:10AM. After turning the water back on, I unpacked just enough, showered, and was in bed after 4AM. I woke up at 10:30AM. Dad only slept until 8am because of the mowers outside. We went to town after drinking our coffee. Went to HEB, got ice, convenience store, then mowed the lawn. It was out of control. The grass was so tall. We had 4 inches of rain while we were gone. I worked out a little after. We just ate cauliflower pizza and showering soon. Literally just got back home and ready to leave again already. I miss Italy. Carpe Diem.

1:25PM   10.19.23   Texas

Yesterday was a blur, just as today has been so far. It is always easier to fill up a journal when you are actually doing things with your life and not sitting in the same chair you have been sitting in for the last three years. I hate it, but such is life. We cannot always be on the go. Sometimes, we must suffer for a duration of time to achieve the next phase of life, the new beginning of a journey. After finishing up yesterday, dad and I ate our pizza, watched the same TV shows we had been watching when we left for Italy. We finished up Virgin River season 5, then watched, "American Made" with Tom Cruise. It is such a great movie. I have watched it three or four times. Houston beat the Rangers last night, making the series 2-1, Rangers. I was in bed by 10:30PM and fell asleep around 11:30PM. I woke up before 10AM. I had my coffee, watched GetUp!, then went and ran 2 miles on the track. 2.5 miles by the time I got back to the house. dad was dressed before I left and needed to go into town. I finished my work out before 11:45AM. We drove to Wal-Mart, spent another $80.00 on water, Gatorade, protein shakes, laundry detergent. It is fucking insnane what it costs to simply stay alive here in the states. I honestly have zero idea as to how families are making it. I remember my mom buying groceries for us as kids. $200-$300 would last about a month, if not longer. Now, people are spending that a week. a lot of new projects on the horizon for me. exciting times ahead with what is in store. Carpe Diem.

12:08PM   10.21.23   Texas

With this last page, I am trying to find the words needed to show my appreciation for my brother, for making this trip possible. I was not sure how I would hold up on the plane rides, being in a different country for a long period of time, and being sick for over a week once I got there, all without having my anxiety flare up. The longest flight I had been on prior to these were the ones we took when I was in the Marines and we went to Afghanistan. They were all double digit hours, but we were all taking Nyquil and sleeping through it. My anxiety was non-existent up until I got out of the Marines in 2010. After the panic attack in 2013 that put me in the hospital, it has always been there. But the five hour flight to JFK, the 2 hour flight to Salt Lake City to begin the trip, and then the eight plus hour flights to and from Milan, it all went smoothly. Italy changed me forever. I will always deal with it, but it will not control me or my life. being back in Texas since the seventeenth, I can honestly feel the change, the difference the trip as a whole has made on me. Be afraid, but do not let it steer your life. We are the captains of our own destiny. Believe it, and enjoy the ride, the views, and discoveries. Carpe Diem.

4:30PM   10.16.23   SLC

Maybe all we will ever be is a forgotten thought, a conversation never had. to say i think of you every second, would be the equivalent of every clock in the world being stuck, frozen, and holding onto the same set of numbers for the duration of life itself. Each time my lungs surrender a breath, I want your air to call them home. This human I am and have become, does not work properly without your eyes leading me closer to you. I forget how to laugh, cry, smile, and engage in any form of emotion when i am my own prisoner, and you have the key. I am extreme, but only when it comes to you and this all-consuming thought of making sure when I get the chance to hold you, I do not hold on too tight, but still wrapping myself up in your blessings and colorful signs. I am feral, even with your own frailty of hope and shrine. you are the darkness of my light, but home for me has never been ignited before you. Your warmth is my beginning, a poem integrated with your moans. If I am anything, it is only because of you. It is only when you tell me how much of yourself was found with my help, and you helping me find what I thought I had lost before my parents divorced, do I realize the kind of love that exists in this version of reality. You are Eden, the garden, and orchard.

5:20PM   10.1.23   SLC

CONVERGING, COLLIDING

when i think of love, i close my eyes and not only see
your face, your eyes shine from the moon. i am at a

place in my yearly turn from the soul and bone, to a
place where home has a single number tied to the

fingers of you and i, connected until all flesh is
stripped and has been given back to the earth in a sign

of acceptance for who we have always been. we are
humans seeking housing for what disturbs us the most.

4:08PM   10.1.23   SLC

<u>MUSE & LOVER</u>

it has felt like one long day of memories, eating,
laughing, and feeling the fall for the first time this year.
the wind, colors, energy, the entire state of Utah is
magical. it is why i love it here and miss it as much as i
do. where i am sitting on my brother's porch, you can
see the mountainous horizon, the changing foliage, and
bluest of blue skies mixed with cotton balls for clouds.

time has slowed down while we have been here as well.
being an hour behind now tends to do that, but this
place makes you pay attention in a different way than
anywhere i have been. it is in the low 60's, with cooler
temperatures coming later this evening. tomorrow, rain
is being called for in the early morning hours.

not ideal conditions to catch a flight, but where we are
heading, it will not matter to me at all. being here for
over twenty-four hours, it already has me wanting to
come back to live in this state again. everyone is
outside being active, talking, and acting friendly in
their own ways. one more sleep until Italy, but for now,
Utah is my muse and lover.

11:56AM   10.3.23   Saronno

SARONNO

i am out of my element here, but the beauty here is
relentless with its gaze. strangers in a place where one
look turns your eyes into some distant collection of art

to hang in the sky. this is a place of dreamers, artists,
anyone looking for something greater than themselves.
there is so much to see, do, and partake in while we are
here. the weather feels similar to where we just came

from. there are all kinds of humans here. followers of
a different kind of path, all on their own journey. i have
caught eyes with a few today who have given me a new
musing to fit onto a page. the stillness that laid with

their bodies, handed my soul and spine shivers and
almost crumbled me into the thousands of bricks that
are beneath my feet. listen to the wind, breeze, and
small spaces next to you when you search for
something more than who you are.

love is nothing more than taking a first step into the
deepest part of a life you are unfamiliar with.

6:23PM   10.4.23   Lake Como

GILATO & COMO

this part of Italy is old generational, born from the
blood of those before the ones today. being an
American here, you get the looks, the stares, the dirty
eye, as if you are trespassing on everything they have
built and made for themselves. we are staying in a
house that was the man's childhood home. every house
here i would venture to say is that way. it is one
gigantic spiderweb of walk-ways, paths, stairs, and
alleys. each day begins when the church bell next to us
goes off at seven in the morning. it rings every hour
until nine at night. between the bells, traffic is non-stop
next to this house. a road barely wide enough for two
vehicles, with a sidewalk extending halfway down to
the town of, Nesso, where we get our supplies for the
day. i have never felt more like i do not belong
somewhere than walking these streets. we had gilato
earlier. it was as good as i had hoped it would be. i had
an Americano to wash it down. this is one of the most
beautiful places of the world i have ever been to.
my first taste of the Italian life is one of which i will
never forget. this is the perfect getaway, but unless you
speak the language, know someone here, or have your
own vehicle, it is all madness. the experience itself will
change me for the better and allow my writing to grow
even more with time.

12:29PM   1.1.24   Texas

Happy New Year!!

i hope today you feel as if you have what you

need to begin the new year the way you need

it. may the love you seek follow the

light you give off. may your own love

keep you company first.

12:21PM   1.2.24   Texas

do not bend yourself to only fit into

someone's shadow. if they want you in

their life, they will show you. they will

never make you wonder if they are in need

of you when needing you becomes something

they do once they have control of you.

1:36PM   1.3.24   Texas

I wanted to touch your face today,

but I have not spoken to you in three

days. My message still says, sent, left on

read. It is why this will not work. It is why

the small things will never matter to you

when you cannot care enough about any of it.

1:13PM   1.4.24   Texas

Take inventory of your life. Make sure you

know whomever is in your life, that they are

adding to it. Be sure you know who is taking

away without being present in yours. We are

not harbors. We are destinations. We are

worthy of remembering that.

2:44PM   1.5.24   Texas

Make your own life the priority. Do whatever you can

to surround yourself with positive energy and a blissful

outlook. Your life depends on what you let go of,

because if you do not, you will find out how deep

sorrow is and learn that the abyss is nothing more than

staring back into your own light, wondering where you

went when leaving behind everything that mattered.

1:22PM　　　　　　1.6.24　　　　　　Texas

When your life is not what you want it to be,

you must take inventory of what it is. Correct it.

Focus on it. Invest in what you need it to be.

Make sure you have yourself at the front of your

life's line. You cannot afford to put anyone in

front of you at this point of your journey.

You will always matter, too.

11:47AM   1.7.24   Texas

We are the dreams living in our bodily forms.

Where our hearts go, love will shield us from the pain,

or at least we hope it will. Not everything will make

sense to you in this lifetime. You will find yourself

questioning each and every thing you do at some point.

You must lean into your own understanding and not

follow a crowd when the only direction they know is

how to get back to the wolves.

1:57PM   1.8.24   Texas

Another day left wondering where I stand with
someone. If they do not respect you enough to
message you back after a week, it is time to let
go and make room for more of yourself. It should
not even take a day for them to reply, knowing where
they stand in your life. To understand a narcissist,
you must know they will do everything in their
power to make you feel as though you are in the
wrong and downplay the act of sabotage they are
demonstrating. They will spend their entire life
trying to take and regain the power they lost
after they finally meet someone who does not
tolerate their incompetence and abuse.

1:58PM   1.8.24   Texas

One day, it will not take someone longer to think

of you than you think of them. One day, someone

will show you why you were left feeling alone all

those times you needed someone to close the

distance with yourself. in our lifetime, we will

meet a handful of those who can sit with us when

it's the last thing we want to do for ourselves.

Forever happens daily with them.

12:47PM   1.9.24   Texas

Be cautious of those who want more from you on days

you feel as though you are doing more than enough.

There is a limit we all reach. I found mine a few days

ago with you. There will always be those we write

about and are forced to leave behind. I just hope when

they open the book, they will be able to know and feel

the love they hope to find one day, does exist and can

be found if you look in the right places.

2:52PM   1.10.24   Texas

To truly be ourselves and choose our own space

is the main objective in this lifetime. Anything else

and you are keeping your life from becoming the

dream itself. You will never find yourself settling

when you know what it took and how many lives

you lost getting here today.

2:17PM   1.11.24   Texas

Beware of the negativity of your own mind.

We can only do and accomplish so much within

a day. Learn to love who you are, instead of blaming

yourself for things not working out. There will be days

when you will not feel like yourself. It is on those days

you must show up for the child in you who never had

anyone there to fight for them. Protect your soul by

advancing your peace, move by move.

2:22PM   1.12.24   Texas

Do not take this life and believe you have to follow

the rules. Creatives will always write, draw, or speak

a new world into existence. It is there that love is born

for self and the creation itself. We will draw in the

sun when there is not one to be found. We will paint

in the moon when her light fades beyond the eyes of

a dreamer. We will write about a love that we may

never find just to make the pain feel as though it is

a momentary and temporary thing. We do not

follow the lines, because we are the rule and

the maker of our own.

11:07AM   1.14.24   Texas

Love your life. Love your path. Love your growth.

Take care of your mental health as well. We can only

control so much, attitude and change. Take charge of

it, because the quality of your life depends on it.

I finally had to let go of you, of it all, to remember

what my hands could do once they healed from the

violence, grief, and everyday anxiety. I am learning,

but it still hurts even thinking about more days of it

consuming me. But I must if I am to move on for good.

2:05PM   1.15.24   Texas

I think about you it seems like every single day.

I wonder who else has someone like that, more so

about someone they are not with. You have buried

yourself inside of my heart and mind, an endless trench

system of your memory, trench warfare. A love loss,

but a muse gained. You are the first breath in the

morning, between inceptions and lucid. You are the

touch I try to write about, that I still try to remember.

2:41PM   1.17.24   Texas

Happy Day 17.

I thought I had journaled yesterday, but I forgot and

thought I'd write something to the degree of our minds

needing rest. Do not overdo or over-extend yourself,

because in reality, it can wait. Regardless of how much

you believe everything will fall apart, your mind will

be your greatest enemy once you believe in the

negative light it can oftentimes live and breed in.

Breathe. Release. Rest. Try again tomorrow.

2:11PM   1.18.24   Texas

The more I think about it, the less I feel I need to tell
you. As the days pass, the months welcome new years

and feelings. I still miss you and I fucking hate
knowing I always will. When we first began talking,

I knew you would always be a part of me in some
capacity. It is why letting you go in full was never in

the plans for me. It was never an option for me,
because once you meet someone who can look at you

as if you aren't the monster you once thought yourself
to, the more love pours out of your wounds instead of
the blood that never felt safe in your own body.

12:08PM   1.19.24   Texas

We will never truly love until we see ourselves the way

others do. Some of us are better off being in the

shadows, full off of the light. It is there we find that

darkness is capable of being a nurturer, a holding hand

when everything else around us becomes wilted limbs.

2:02PM   1.20.24   Texas

We become the best versions of ourselves after

realizing we will be the only love we will ever get back

the same way we give it. Take your time with the

process. Sometimes, twenty-four hours is nothing more

than a minute when we understand the value of our

time. Do not be afraid to hope for me, to look towards

the open spaces and see growth on the horizon.

12:24PM   1.21.24   Texas

I lost a friend the other day to suicide. Today is her
birthday. Four days ago, her daughter turned twelve.
I wish I had the money to go back to college and
become a therapist/psychologist. I was made to help
others. I hope in her last moments, she knew how much
she was loved. I hope it is quiet and calm for her now.
We never know what someone is going through, and
probably will never know, but it shouldn't keep us from
reaching out to make sure we did all we could to help,
even if asking themselves is the furthest thing from
their minds at the time. I feel sorry for the hurt that so
many of us feel as though we cannot talk about. Some
of us got lucky and only have scars to show for the
exact moments ending it all felt better than breathing
more air into these lungs of ours.

2:44PM   1.22.24   Texas

Another journal filled. This is the fourth one I have

done from the ones I bought in Italy and the ones I

brought with me while I was there. I am saving certain

ones to use when I start traveling again. I cannot wait.

I feel it will be soon. Find what you love. Love it

dearly. Make sure it never feels neglected. Our gifts are

the children we once were that almost didn't survive.

2:30PM   10.12.23   JFK

-JFK-

Sitting at the airport, drinking Dunkin' Donuts coffee, watching people do what they do when they come to the airport. Everyone is different, their own unique symbolic stamp of what makes them human and what separates them from everyone else. We are all so busy with our lives, we forget who we are when we go out of the place we remain for so long. I think it is a beautiful thing when someone locks eyes with me here. You do not get a lot of that these days. Everyone is either looking down at their phones, shoes, and everywhere else but towards the person in front of them. Maybe, one day, we will have a singular reason besides being in love with someone when looking at a stranger you might have more in common with than you think in this lifetime. Maybe curiosity is frowned upon because no one likes to be judged. I would rather you judge and look at me, than not and pretend you know me when your eyes finally do meet mine in some timid form of acknowledgment when I catch you looking up through your hands, which are covering your yawn and shine.

11:10AM   10.13.23   SLC

-AUTUMN IN UTAH-

Maybe I was born to be broken, but love still holds this soul open and wide. Fresh air here, colors painting the fall, blue skies fill the void of where the darkness once covered these eyes. If I could be anywhere with anything these days, I do not know if I would need anything more than I have right now with anything more than I do not have right now. When being alone fits the mode of sensation and euphoria, you seek it out in every place you go. Being here now, I realize just how much I have missed everything about this place. The weather alone makes magic gravitate to the soil, eyes, passerby, and all the empty spots not colored in by the oranges, yellows, and reds. This crispness creates a crease down the center of my spine, branching out for glory, and all things I have come to find love to be a part of. With or without you by my side, I will gladly take my own shadow enlarging the parts of stone and pine to where there are only my ambitions taking up the slack you left behind.

4:57PM   10.13.23   SLC

-PARK CITY LIVING-

Calico autumn, crazed and deranged expectations of what we want versus what we need. I am a too far off the bone kind of soul, rugged and versed in holy wars and homeless scriptures. There are a few out here living well beyond their means, biting off more than they can chew with their golden and ivory teeth. Defenders, Broncos, Porsches, Audis, and Mercedes take up every lane on the road, and all I know is how to walk a line for cheap, with mud and blood on my elbows and knees. Maybe if the sun hit me just right, you could see that I still have color in my eyes. No pain exists quite like that of the absence you get once hope for love leaves you after being your entire life since you were an orphaned kid. Women walk with nothing but designer on their arms, even with their man attached and holding a hand, they look at you as if they could afford you, too. I do my best not to stare or even notice their eyes, because all mine see are goodbyes and lonely times. I am not sure there is anything good left about me that she didn't already take with her. I am not sure there is anything you could want to get to know about me. Finding myself in coffee shops, where my people exist, where the wanderers can be found, I sip my Americano and watch the world turn around. Only then, can I see myself and someone else wondering about me as I do with them, and how quickly I could fall for a woman out here who only has a quiet life attached to them.

3:41PM   10.16.23   SLC

-PANIC STAGES-

I wish I didn't have to deal with my anxiety as much as I do. Some days, it hibernates within these caved in bones, resting and preparing for the next stalk. Other days, I forget it is there, like a single wave passing through the ocean's heart, quiet and simple with leniency. Today, out of nowhere, I felt a panic attack come over me. I wish I understood the psyche better or the true psychological side of those triggers. I am sure it had something to do with being as high up as we were in the mountains and feeling as if both sides were going to crush me. It happened once before when I went to Mt. Zion several years ago. Once I am out of the vehicle, I am perfectly fine. Being in an airplane does not bother me, but the panic is real when I feel trapped between the movable and immovable. Maybe it was the few sips of Red Bull I had before the trek. Maybe it was all in my fucking head. I was able to calm my BPM from the spike of 140bpm down into the 80s eventually. The day was still a very successful one. Beauty always wins in the end.

3:57PM   10.16.23   SLC

-ALTA-

On the road is where I find my "why." It is between the lines of yellow and white I find the divine of all things alive, of all things timely, of all things richly and poorly made. The pristine foliage on the mountainside is everything artists hope to discover when inspiration is our holy sign. It's a sign of the times. It's a sign of divine intervention. It's the road sign with 9mm bullet holes shot between the O and P. It's a fine line walked by madmen and folklore all coming together to uncover and peel back the layers of this earth to find where the treasures are buried and how to implement a new plan to hide them all over again. Immersing yourself with fall, with elevation, with all the elements is where you find out who you are, versus who you have known yourself to be. Being one with the mountains is better than sex for me. It encapsulates all aspects of life, death, rebirth, matrimony, and intercourse on a spiritual level. Reminding yourself daily and constantly exactly how slight, insignificant, and unimportant you are is the best teacher for remaining grounded, healed, opened, and humbled. Existing between two mountains, just for a few seconds, puts you in your place abruptly and quickly, wihtout hesitation. Conceding to the elements around you, provides you a distinct outlet of confessing all of the lies you tell yourself on a daily basis. Staring out into the valleys of pine, ash, snow, and boulders, all infinitely times as big as you are, allows for a soulful acclimation for the body you are. Out there, you are nothing more than bones, flesh, doubts, and fears for the wolves to eat, dying with nothing but a name you go by for others to remember who you were. Being true to your purpose means figuring out why you do not fit in where you are today. My confessions feel more honest out here. I can wake up before the sun and hear my guardian angels tell me, "This is the real you. This is where you belong. This is where you make amends for the wrongs you have done and accept the wrongs that have been done to you." I am at peace with how the light reflects more than particles of dust and embers out here. There is harmony found within the steps we take on these untraveled trails and pathways. More so than anywhere I have ever been before. I have zero doubts when the moon peeks her eyes over the horizon to see how her children are getting along. I am a somebody out here, even if it is only me in my life, at least I know my acceptance has finally been received. At least I know what self-love feels like when you don't have to bleed it out to show it. At least I know what happiness is when waking up in a bed, in a state, in a humbly grace served with freshly brewed coffee and panoramic views. I have not gotten a lot of things right in my life, but getting out of my head to live here has been my greatest decision.

4:13PM   10.16.23   SLC

-A SHADOW NOT BELONGING TO ME-

I know there is another place I am supposed to be. I know being unable to leave my father's side has kept me from being with someone I love and unable to travel as often as I would like. Sacrifice takes on an entirely new set of eyes and skin when your life is nothing but doing the same routine, day in and day out. Sitting here on my brother's deck/porch area, looking out and seeing the mountain in front of me reaching its hands up and touching the sky, with fall slipping out of its coma further each day. I become even more enamored with the word and feeling of freedom by following through on a conviction and promise I made myself years ago that when it's time to uproot and go, you must go. I have not had much of a life to speak of the last four years. I did my best to maximize these two weeks and gather every single fucking moment, memory, and experience I could to replace the vast emptiness and gorge my existence has been shrouded by to make up for the lost time I feel I am made up of. The cold truth is, my father has become a weighted entanglement of humanity within my own ambitions and desires. Love is a weird thing, even more so with family. We do not know who we are with them around. We forget our own needs exist.

NEVER

BEFORE

SEEN

WRITINGS

8:58PM   8.11.24   Texas

We all suffer for the love we want, but rarely get back

in return. The hope is enough to kill us, mangle us,

and push us off of the ledge we have been clinging

onto since the day we found out what life could be

like once a heart is exchanged for poetry. Through it

all, even the ache of knowing it is out there, we are

still here, kicking, screaming, living, and creating

art that without, would have killed us the day we

found out it was nothing but a child's game played

by adults who waste more time than any creature ever

has before in the history of space and colliding energy.

2:28PM   4.25.24   Texas

-BE YOURSELF FOR LOVE-

I hold you like the promise you are, the soul of the cosmos you have been, and the shadow that comforts my shadow so beautifully. If there is ever a day without you in my thoughts, I will know where to go to find you. You are a tiny thing, but you take up all of me. You are a mystic inception of roses and doves, resting and reverting back to the sky underneath me and the earth above me. There is no prayer without your amen at the beginning and end. There is no cathedral without your windows and unhinged light sneaking in. Hold steady, sweet reverie. Be relentless with me and with anything you end up loving beyond the name and recognition it could provide you if you lose yourself amongst its courage and credence.

11:03AM   5.22.19   St. George, UT

The only time I ever wish to feel this kind of heartache again is when I am only my deathbed, knowing I will be gone while she continues on, being the most incredible woman to ever walk, run, and fly beside me. When she is turning as young as eighty and as old as the love we made and had together, that is how I will respond to anyone who asks me what love is like when it is with the right human. They take away a past which you once had to become an alcoholic to forget. At least for me, love dried me out in the best of ways.

9:06PM   11.22.22   Mimi's House

These walls have bled dry of the tears I have cried against them, wondering if there would ever come a time when the pain would end. Love becomes a cage if you believe you can leave when you want. Your wings will persih, fall by the wayside and into the night. There is no wrong way to live, but only to live without fear of loving often, to live as a bird who knows what cages do to their songs and stature.

11:52AM   8.27.24   Texas

You are the backbone vulnerability stands with. If you know her, you will be able to find her sitting with her legs crossed in the grass, away from everything except coffee and a book she has read a few times, but goes back to find the parts she had underlined and marked in yellow as an important part of her own story. When she cannot find herself in life, she finds herself in the words others have offered, knowingly or unknowingly, as a haven for wanderlusts like her.

9:50AM   12.3.23   Texas

It's easy to decipher your silence. I have been around it my entire life. My mother used it on me when there was only one beer left to silent her demons. She taught me how to love a darkness no one else wanted at a tender age of six. She taught me how saying nothing was an endearment learned from those who showed her the same treatment. I know if you could reach out, you would. I no longer get annoyed or frustrated by someone's negligence when the only control I have is that of my own anger as it pertains to humans who have never known themselves beyond their teenage years.

8:32PM   11.29.23   Texas

-SEASON OF MISUNDERSTANDING-

I wish I could hold you closer than winter holds these bones of mine during a season of cold and shivers breaking my face in-half and causing a landslide of emotions to pour over what is left of a writer's life. Do I shake the trees inside of you as you do for me? My nature is still healing, still reeling, but I feel each one of your winged footsteps crunch the dead limbs from the last time a gatherer attempted to console what love left behind. I do not wish to be anyone more than who you need me to be for this part of your life. I do not do well when it comes to patience and waiting for hands and eyes to hold mine the same way. I know if you want something in life, you will have to die before it shares how it felt about you. You will have to wait until you are freshly lowered down into the dirt before your flowers are received. The only thing left is the muse when a poet dedicates his life to a love that never gets returned. What a gift it must be to never die and be loved for the heart that provided comfort to the dark parts of a human dying to be heard.

12:57PM   8.8.24   Texas

-LION'S GATE-

To the woman wearing yellow, may your eyes only water the flowers you collect for the gardens of guardians protecting your doors and walls. Every word I write feels like it could have been your exact emotion in a past life. You are a wild child of the most holy, a signature hallelujah designed by Cohen, and the gold and sapphire used by Monet to paint what others never had the patience to sit with long enough to see. I have never witnessed a combination of flesh and bone like yours before. A royalty of soul depicted by abstract light, with cobalt violet peeking through feverish sunsets. You may ask me what I want from this, and I would simply say, to write you into every life after this.

www.ingramcontent.com/pod-product-compliance
Lightning Source LLC
Chambersburg PA
CBHW012024110726
47994CB00012B/3294